Capitalizing on Post-Global Warming Opportunities

Copyright Page

TITLE: Capitalizing on Post-Global Warming Opportunities

1ST Edition

ISBN: 9798223131960

Capitalizing on Post-Global Warming Opportunities

By Roberto Miguel Rodriguez

Chapter 1: Canada and Russia: The Big Winners in the Post-Global Warming World?

The Changing Arctic: An Introduction to the Impact of Global Warming on the Arctic Region

The Arctic region is undergoing significant changes as a result of global warming. The melting ice is opening up new opportunities and challenges for countries like Canada and Russia. In this subchapter, we will explore the various ways in which these nations can capitalize on the post-global warming world.

Arctic resource extraction is one area where both Canada and Russia can benefit immensely. With the increased accessibility of natural resources due to melting ice, mining, oil and gas extraction, and other resource-based industries can flourish. This presents an opportunity for economic growth and development.

Another avenue for growth is renewable energy development. Canada and Russia have vast potential for wind, solar, and hydroelectric power generation. By tapping into these resources, they can become leaders in clean energy production, contributing to a sustainable future.

The changing Arctic environment also presents opportunities in the tourism industry. As the effects of global warming become more evident, tourists are increasingly interested in witnessing the unique environmental changes and wildlife in the Arctic regions. Canada and Russia can attract these tourists, boosting their economies and promoting environmental awareness.

The melting ice also opens up new fishing grounds and opportunities for aquaculture. Canada and Russia can expand their fishing industries and meet the growing global demand for seafood. This presents an avenue for economic growth while ensuring sustainable fishing practices.

Infrastructure development and shipping routes are also crucial in the post-global warming world. With the opening of new Arctic shipping routes, Canada and Russia can invest in ports and shipping lanes to facilitate increased trade and transportation between Europe and Asia. This can lead to improved economic integration and connectivity.

Research and scientific collaboration are vital in understanding and addressing the challenges posed by climate change. Canada and Russia can collaborate on research initiatives focused on climate change, adaptation strategies, and environmental preservation. This will not only advance scientific knowledge but also foster international cooperation.

Both Canada and Russia can take advantage of emerging carbon offset markets by investing in carbon capture and storage technologies, offering carbon credits, and participating in emissions trading. This will not only help combat climate change but also provide economic opportunities.

As the effects of global warming become more pronounced, Canada and Russia can develop and export expertise in climate change adaptation and resilience planning to other nations facing similar challenges. This can contribute to global efforts in building resilience and adapting to a changing climate.

Preserving indigenous land management practices and traditional knowledge is essential in the face of climate change. Canada and Russia can support indigenous communities in maintaining their cultural heritage while promoting sustainable land-use practices.

With increased economic and geopolitical interests in the Arctic region, Canada and Russia can play a significant role in shaping international agreements, regulations, and governance frameworks related to Arctic affairs. This presents an opportunity for both nations to demonstrate leadership and influence in the global arena.

The changing Arctic is not just a challenge; it is also an opportunity for Canada and Russia. By capitalizing on the post-global warming world, these countries can foster economic growth, promote sustainability, and shape the future of the Arctic region.

The Economic Potential: Understanding the Opportunities for Canada and Russia

In the rapidly changing post-global warming world, Canada and Russia are emerging as the big winners, harnessing the economic potential that the Arctic region offers. With melting ice opening up new possibilities, both countries can capitalize on a range of opportunities that will shape their future prosperity.

Arctic resource extraction is at the forefront of economic development for Canada and Russia. The increased accessibility of natural resources, such as mining, oil, and gas, presents a significant advantage. Both countries can tap into these resources, driving economic growth and creating job opportunities in resource-based industries.

The shift towards renewable energy sources also presents a unique opportunity for Canada and Russia. With their vast potential for wind, solar, and hydroelectric power generation, they can become leaders in clean energy production. By embracing renewable energy, both countries can reduce their reliance on fossil fuels and contribute to mitigating climate change.

Tourism and ecotourism are another avenue for economic growth. As global warming continues to reshape the Arctic environment, Canada and Russia can attract tourists interested in witnessing the unique environmental changes and wildlife in these regions. This sector can contribute to local economies and foster a greater understanding of the importance of environmental preservation.

The melting Arctic ice also brings new fishing grounds and opportunities for aquaculture. Canada and Russia can expand their fishing industries to meet the growing global demand for seafood. By responsibly managing these resources, they can ensure sustainable fishing practices and contribute to food security.

Infrastructure development and shipping routes are crucial for facilitating increased trade and transportation between Europe and Asia. As new Arctic shipping routes open up, both countries can invest in ports and shipping lanes. This will not only boost their own economies but also promote international trade and collaboration.

The changing climate in the Arctic presents an opportunity for Canada and Russia to collaborate on research initiatives. By focusing on climate change, adaptation strategies, and environmental preservation, they can lead the way in scientific advancements and foster international cooperation.

Both Canada and Russia can take advantage of emerging carbon offset markets by investing in carbon capture and storage technologies. This will allow them to offer carbon credits and participate in emissions trading, contributing to global efforts to combat climate change.

As the effects of global warming become more pronounced, Canada and Russia can develop and export expertise in climate change adaptation and resilience planning. By sharing their knowledge and experiences, they can help other nations facing similar challenges and create new economic opportunities.

Preserving indigenous land management practices and traditional knowledge is of utmost importance in the face of climate change. Canada and Russia can support these practices, fostering cultural preservation and sustainable land-use practices that benefit both indigenous communities and the environment.

Lastly, with increased economic and geopolitical interests in the Arctic region, Canada and Russia can play a significant role in shaping international agreements, regulations, and governance frameworks. By actively engaging in Arctic diplomacy, they can ensure the sustainable and responsible development of the region.

In conclusion, the economic potential for Canada and Russia in the post-global warming world is vast. By capitalizing on opportunities in resource extraction, renewable energy, tourism, fisheries, infrastructure development, research collaboration, carbon offset markets, adaptation strategies, indigenous land management, and Arctic diplomacy, both countries can secure their positions as leaders in the changing global landscape.

Chapter 2: Arctic resource extraction

Melting Ice: How Increased Accessibility is Transforming Resource Extraction in the Arctic

In the subchapter "Melting Ice: How Increased Accessibility is Transforming Resource Extraction in the Arctic," we delve into the opportunities that Canada and Russia can seize in the post-global warming world. This chapter is dedicated to politicians, educators, journalists, the public, and anyone interested in the potential benefits of the changing Arctic landscape.

Arctic resource extraction is a key focus, as the melting ice opens up new possibilities for mining, oil and gas extraction, and other resource-based industries. Both Canada and Russia are poised to benefit from the increased accessibility of natural resources in the Arctic region. The abundance of these resources presents an opportunity for economic growth and job creation in these nations.

Furthermore, the shift towards renewable energy sources allows Canada and Russia to tap into their vast potential for wind, solar, and hydroelectric power generation. By becoming leaders in clean energy production, they can contribute to combating climate change while also capitalizing on the growing demand for renewable energy.

The unique environmental changes and wildlife in the Arctic regions can also attract tourists. Canada and Russia can develop their tourism and ecotourism sectors, offering visitors the chance to witness the effects of global warming firsthand. This not only boosts their economies but also raises awareness about the importance of environmental preservation.

As the Arctic ice continues to melt, new fishing grounds and opportunities for aquaculture emerge. This allows Canada and Russia to expand their fishing industries and meet the growing global demand for seafood. Additionally, the opening of new Arctic shipping routes presents a chance for infrastructure development. Investments in ports and shipping lanes can facilitate increased trade and transportation between Europe and Asia, benefiting both nations.

The changing climate in the Arctic also calls for research and scientific collaboration. Canada and Russia can work together to study climate change, develop adaptation strategies, and preserve the environment. They can also take advantage of the emerging carbon offset markets, investing in carbon capture and storage technologies, offering carbon credits, and participating in emissions trading.

Moreover, Canada and Russia can develop and export expertise in climate change adaptation and resilience planning to other nations facing similar challenges. By sharing their knowledge, they can contribute to global efforts in combating the effects of global warming.

Lastly, both countries can play a significant role in shaping international agreements, regulations, and governance frameworks related to Arctic affairs. With their economic and geopolitical interests in the region, they can lead the way in Arctic diplomacy, ensuring sustainable development and environmental preservation.

In conclusion, the melting ice in the Arctic presents numerous opportunities for Canada and Russia. By embracing these opportunities, they can become major players in the post-global warming world, capitalizing on resource extraction, renewable energy, tourism, fisheries, infrastructure development, research collaboration, carbon offset markets, adaptation strategies, indigenous land management, and Arctic diplomacy.

Mining Opportunities: Exploring Canada and Russia's Potential for Arctic Mineral Extraction

As the effects of global warming continue to reshape the Arctic region, both Canada and Russia find themselves in a unique position to capitalize on the newfound accessibility of natural resources. With melting ice opening up opportunities for mining, oil and gas extraction, and other resource-based industries, these two nations stand to be the big winners in the post-global warming world.

The Arctic region is rich in mineral deposits, including gold, diamonds, rare earth elements, and oil and gas reserves. With the melting ice making these resources more accessible, Canada and Russia can tap into their vast potential for Arctic mineral extraction. This presents an unprecedented opportunity for economic growth and development.

Additionally, as the world shifts towards renewable energy sources, both Canada and Russia can leverage their immense potential for wind, solar, and hydroelectric power generation. By becoming leaders in clean energy production, these nations can not only reduce their reliance on fossil fuels but also contribute to the global transition towards sustainability.

The changing climate in the Arctic also presents an opportunity for Canada and Russia to attract tourists interested in witnessing the unique environmental changes and wildlife in the region. With its breathtaking landscapes and diverse wildlife, the Arctic has the potential to become a popular destination for ecotourism, providing a boost to the local economies.

Furthermore, as the Arctic ice melts, new fishing grounds and opportunities for aquaculture emerge. Canada and Russia can expand their fishing industries to meet the growing global demand for seafood. This not only strengthens their economies but also ensures food security and economic stability for the region.

To facilitate increased trade and transportation between Europe and Asia, Canada and Russia can invest in infrastructure development, such as ports and shipping lanes. The opening of new Arctic shipping routes presents a lucrative opportunity to enhance connectivity and economic cooperation on a global scale.

The changing climate in the Arctic also calls for research and scientific collaboration. Canada and Russia can join forces to study climate change, adaptation strategies, and environmental preservation. Their expertise in these areas can be shared with the international community to address the challenges posed by global warming.

Both Canada and Russia can take advantage of the emerging carbon offset markets by investing in carbon capture and storage technologies, offering carbon credits, and participating in emissions trading. This not only helps combat climate change but also opens up new economic opportunities.

As the effects of global warming become more pronounced, Canada and Russia can develop and export expertise in climate change adaptation and resilience planning to other nations facing similar challenges. By doing so, they can position themselves as leaders in the field of climate change mitigation and contribute to global efforts to build resilience.

In addition, Canada and Russia can support the preservation of indigenous land management practices and traditional knowledge in the face of climate change. By fostering cultural preservation and sustainable land-use practices, they can ensure the long-term sustainability of the Arctic region.

With increased economic and geopolitical interests in the Arctic region, Canada and Russia can play a significant role in shaping international agreements, regulations, and governance frameworks related to Arctic affairs. Their active participation in Arctic diplomacy and governance will be crucial in ensuring sustainable development and effective resource management in the region.

In conclusion, Canada and Russia have a wealth of opportunities to explore in the post-global warming world. From increased mining opportunities to renewable energy development, tourism, fisheries, and aquaculture, these nations can harness their potential to drive economic growth, scientific collaboration, and sustainable development in the Arctic region. By capitalizing on these opportunities, Canada and Russia can position themselves as global leaders in the era of climate change.

Oil and Gas Extraction: Leveraging the Arctic's Energy Reserves for Economic Growth

In the post-global warming world, Canada and Russia have emerged as the big winners in the Arctic region. As the ice continues to melt, both countries can capitalize on the increased accessibility of natural resources in the Arctic, particularly in the areas of mining, oil and gas extraction, and other resource-based industries. This subchapter explores how Canada and Russia can leverage the Arctic's energy reserves for economic growth.

With their vast reserves of oil and gas, Canada and Russia are well-positioned to become leaders in the energy sector. As the world shifts towards renewable energy sources, both countries can tap into their potential for wind, solar, and hydroelectric power generation, establishing themselves as pioneers in clean energy production. This not only contributes to their economic growth but also addresses the global demand for sustainable energy solutions.

Moreover, the changing climate in the Arctic presents an opportunity for Canada and Russia to attract tourists interested in witnessing the unique environmental changes and wildlife in the region. By promoting tourism and ecotourism, both countries can boost their economies while raising awareness about the effects of global warming and the need for environmental preservation.

The melting of Arctic ice also opens up new fishing grounds and opportunities for aquaculture. Canada and Russia can expand their fishing industries and meet the growing global demand for seafood. This not only supports their economies but also contributes to global food security.

To facilitate increased trade and transportation between Europe and Asia, Canada and Russia can invest in infrastructure development, such as ports and shipping lanes. The opening of new Arctic shipping routes presents a significant opportunity for economic growth and increased international trade.

The changing climate in the Arctic necessitates research and scientific collaboration. Canada and Russia can join forces to study climate change, develop adaptation strategies, and preserve the environment. By collaborating on research initiatives, both countries can stay at the forefront of scientific knowledge and contribute to global efforts in addressing climate change.

Additionally, both Canada and Russia can benefit from participating in carbon offset markets and emissions trading. By investing in carbon capture and storage technologies, offering carbon credits, and participating in emissions trading, they can take advantage of emerging market opportunities while addressing climate change.

As the effects of global warming become more pronounced, Canada and Russia can also develop and export expertise in climate change adaptation and resilience planning. Other nations facing similar challenges can benefit from their knowledge and experience, fostering international collaboration and sustainable practices.

Finally, both Canada and Russia have a responsibility to support indigenous land management practices and preserve traditional knowledge in the face of climate change. By respecting and incorporating indigenous perspectives, they can promote cultural preservation and sustainable land-use practices.

In conclusion, Canada and Russia have numerous opportunities for economic growth and global leadership in the Arctic region. By leveraging the energy reserves, embracing renewable energy, promoting tourism, expanding fisheries, investing in infrastructure, fostering research collaboration, participating in carbon offset markets, developing resilience strategies, preserving indigenous knowledge, and shaping Arctic governance, both countries can secure their positions as key players in the post-global warming world.

Other Resource-Based Industries: Diversifying the Arctic Economy through Timber, Diamonds, and More

The Arctic region is not only a treasure trove of natural resources, but also a land of immense opportunities for Canada and Russia to diversify their economies. As the effects of global warming continue to reshape the Arctic landscape, both countries can capitalize on these changes by exploring various resource-based industries. This subchapter delves into the potential of timber, diamonds, and more in driving economic growth in the Arctic.

Timber has long been a valuable resource in both Canada and Russia, and with the melting ice, the availability of timber in the Arctic region is expected to increase. This presents an opportunity for both countries to expand their forestry industries and meet the growing global demand for sustainable timber products. By investing in responsible logging practices and promoting reforestation efforts, Canada and Russia can ensure the long-term viability of this industry while contributing to the fight against climate change.

Additionally, the Arctic is known for its rich deposits of diamonds. With the melting ice, accessing these precious stones becomes easier, opening up new avenues for diamond mining in the region. Canada and Russia, already major players in the global diamond market, can further strengthen their positions by investing in advanced mining technologies and sustainable extraction practices. This would not only boost their economies but also create employment opportunities for local communities.

Moreover, the Arctic region holds potential for other resource-based industries such as rare earth metals, oil shale, and natural gas. By strategically developing these industries, Canada and Russia can tap into new sources of revenue and reduce their dependence on traditional fossil fuels. This would align with the global shift towards renewable energy sources and position both countries as leaders in clean energy production.

Furthermore, the Arctic's unique environmental changes and wildlife make it an attractive destination for tourists interested in ecotourism. Canada and Russia can capitalize on this by promoting sustainable tourism practices and offering visitors the chance to witness the effects of global warming firsthand. This would not only drive economic growth but also raise awareness about the importance of environmental conservation.

In conclusion, the Arctic region offers a plethora of opportunities for Canada and Russia to diversify their economies and capitalize on the post-global warming world. By exploring resource-based industries such as timber, diamonds, and more, both countries can drive economic growth, create employment opportunities, and contribute to sustainable development. However, it is crucial for policymakers, educators, journalists, and the public to understand the importance of responsible resource extraction and the need to preserve the fragile Arctic ecosystem for future generations. Only through careful planning, collaboration, and sustainable practices can Canada and Russia truly become the big winners in the post-global warming world.

Chapter 3: Renewable energy development

The Shift towards Renewable Energy Sources: Implications for Canada and Russia

As the world grapples with the consequences of global warming, the Arctic region presents unique opportunities for both Canada and Russia. In this subchapter, we will explore how the shift towards renewable energy sources can have significant implications for these two nations.

Renewable energy development holds immense potential for both Canada and Russia. With their vast landscapes, Canada and Russia can tap into their abundant wind, solar, and hydroelectric resources, positioning themselves as leaders in clean energy production. By investing in renewable energy technologies, both countries can reduce their reliance on fossil fuels, decrease greenhouse gas emissions, and contribute to global efforts in combating climate change.

Furthermore, the transition towards renewable energy sources can open up new economic avenues for Canada and Russia. Both nations can establish themselves as exporters of clean energy, meeting the growing global demand for sustainable power solutions. This shift can also create jobs, stimulate economic growth, and attract investment in research and development.

Additionally, the effects of global warming present opportunities for Canada and Russia in other sectors as well. The increased accessibility of natural resources in the Arctic region, due to melting ice, allows for expanded mining, oil and gas extraction, and other resource-based industries. This can contribute to economic growth and bolster the countries' resource sectors.

Moreover, the unique environmental changes in the Arctic regions can attract tourists interested in witnessing the impacts of global warming and experiencing the region's diverse wildlife. This presents an opportunity for Canada and Russia to develop their tourism and ecotourism industries, promoting sustainable practices and generating revenue.

As the Arctic ice melts, new fishing grounds and opportunities for aquaculture emerge. Canada and Russia can expand their fishing industries to meet the growing global demand for seafood, while ensuring sustainable fishing practices.

The opening of new Arctic shipping routes also calls for infrastructure development. Both countries can invest in ports and shipping lanes, facilitating increased trade and transportation between Europe and Asia. This presents an opportunity for economic growth and increased connectivity.

The changing climate in the Arctic necessitates research and scientific collaboration. Canada and Russia can work together on initiatives focused on climate change, adaptation strategies, and environmental preservation. This collaboration can lead to innovative solutions and contribute to the global scientific community's understanding of climate change.

Furthermore, both Canada and Russia can take advantage of emerging carbon offset markets and emissions trading. By investing in carbon capture and storage technologies and offering carbon credits, they can participate in these markets and contribute to global efforts in reducing carbon emissions.

The effects of global warming also call for the development and export of expertise in climate change adaptation and resilience planning. Canada and Russia can share their knowledge and strategies with other nations facing similar challenges, fostering international collaboration and creating new economic opportunities.

Lastly, Canada and Russia can support the preservation of indigenous land management practices and traditional knowledge in the face of climate change. This not only fosters cultural preservation but also promotes sustainable land-use practices, ensuring the long-term viability of the Arctic region.

With their increased economic and geopolitical interests in the Arctic region, Canada and Russia can also play a significant role in shaping international agreements, regulations, and governance frameworks related to Arctic affairs. This positions them as influential actors in Arctic diplomacy and governance.

In conclusion, the shift towards renewable energy sources presents numerous implications for Canada and Russia. These implications range from economic opportunities in renewable energy development, resource extraction, tourism, and fisheries, to the fostering of research collaboration, development of adaptation strategies, and preservation of indigenous practices. As these two countries capitalize on post-global warming opportunities, they have the potential to become the big winners in the post-global warming world.

Wind Power Generation: Harnessing the Arctic's Strong Winds for Clean Energy

As the world faces the challenges of climate change, the Arctic region presents unique opportunities for Canada and Russia to become leaders in clean energy production. With the Arctic experiencing the effects of global warming at an accelerated rate, the strong winds in this region can be harnessed to generate renewable energy through wind power.

Harnessing the power of wind in the Arctic has immense potential. The Arctic's strong and consistent winds can be utilized to generate clean energy on a large scale. Both Canada and Russia, with their vast territories in the Arctic, can tap into this potential and become pioneers in wind power generation.

Wind power offers several advantages. It is a clean and renewable energy source, producing no greenhouse gas emissions or air pollutants. By shifting towards wind power, Canada and Russia can reduce their reliance on fossil fuels and contribute to global efforts to combat climate change.

Furthermore, wind power generation can bring about economic benefits. The development of wind farms in the Arctic can create jobs and stimulate local economies. It can also attract investments and promote technological advancements in renewable energy technologies.

To fully capitalize on the Arctic's wind power potential, Canada and Russia must invest in the necessary infrastructure. This includes the construction of wind turbines and transmission lines, as well as the development of energy storage systems to ensure a continuous supply of clean energy.

In addition, governments and industry stakeholders should collaborate to address any potential concerns related to wind power generation in the Arctic. This includes mitigating the impact on wildlife and ensuring that projects are designed and implemented in an environmentally responsible manner.

By harnessing the Arctic's strong winds for clean energy, Canada and Russia can not only reduce their carbon footprint but also position themselves as leaders in renewable energy development. This will not only benefit their economies but also contribute to the global transition towards a sustainable and low-carbon future.

In conclusion, wind power generation in the Arctic presents an opportunity for Canada and Russia to tap into their vast potential for clean energy production. By harnessing the strong winds in this region, both countries can contribute to mitigating climate change, creating economic opportunities, and becoming global leaders in renewable energy development.

Solar Power Generation: Unleashing the Arctic's Potential for Solar Energy

As the world grapples with the challenges of climate change and the transition to renewable energy, the Arctic region presents a unique opportunity for Canada and Russia to become leaders in solar power generation. The melting ice in the Arctic has opened up new possibilities for harnessing solar energy, and both countries are well-positioned to capitalize on this potential.

Solar power is a clean and sustainable energy source that can significantly reduce greenhouse gas emissions and combat climate change. The Arctic, with its long summer days and extended periods of sunlight, offers ideal conditions for solar energy production. By investing in solar power infrastructure, both Canada and Russia can tap into this vast potential and contribute to the global shift towards renewable energy.

Politicians, educators, journalists, and the public must recognize the numerous benefits of solar power generation in the Arctic. Firstly, it can provide a reliable and sustainable source of energy, reducing dependence on fossil fuels and promoting energy security. Moreover, solar power can stimulate economic growth by creating jobs in the installation, maintenance, and manufacturing of solar panels and related equipment.

Additionally, solar energy can help mitigate the environmental impacts of resource extraction in the Arctic. As both Canada and Russia seek to capitalize on the increased accessibility of natural resources due to melting ice, solar power can offset the carbon emissions associated with mining, oil and gas extraction, and other resource-based industries. It presents an opportunity to develop a diversified and sustainable energy portfolio that balances economic growth with environmental stewardship.

Furthermore, solar power generation in the Arctic can contribute to the region's tourism and ecotourism industries. As the effects of global warming become more evident, tourists are increasingly interested in witnessing the unique environmental changes and wildlife in the Arctic regions. Solar energy infrastructure can serve as a visible symbol of the region's commitment to sustainability and attract environmentally conscious tourists.

To unleash the Arctic's potential for solar energy, Canada and Russia must invest in research and development, policy frameworks, and infrastructure. Collaboration between the two countries on scientific research initiatives focused on solar energy and climate change can accelerate progress in this field. Additionally, governments should provide incentives and support for the deployment of solar power technologies, such as tax credits, subsidies, and streamlined permitting processes.

By seizing the opportunities presented by solar power generation in the Arctic, Canada and Russia can not only contribute to global efforts to combat climate change but also position themselves as leaders in clean energy production. The Arctic boom can extend beyond resource extraction to encompass a sustainable and prosperous future driven by renewable energy.

Hydroelectric Power Generation: Utilizing the Arctic's Abundant Water Resources for Renewable Energy

As the effects of global warming continue to reshape the Arctic landscape, Canada and Russia find themselves at the forefront of a new era of opportunities. One of the most promising avenues for both nations lies in the harnessing of the Arctic's abundant water resources for hydroelectric power generation. With vast rivers and lakes, the Arctic region offers immense potential for clean, renewable energy production.

Hydroelectric power generation has long been recognized as a sustainable and reliable source of energy. By capitalizing on the Arctic's natural water resources, Canada and Russia can become leaders in the global transition towards clean energy. The melting ice in the Arctic has opened up new possibilities for the construction of hydroelectric dams, which can tap into the powerful flow of rivers and generate electricity at a large scale.

By investing in hydroelectric power generation, both countries can reduce their reliance on fossil fuels and significantly contribute to the global fight against climate change. Furthermore, the development of hydroelectric infrastructure in the Arctic can create jobs, stimulate economic growth, and enhance energy security in these nations. The benefits go beyond just environmental sustainability; hydroelectric power can be a catalyst for social and economic development in the Arctic regions.

Additionally, the utilization of hydroelectric power can complement other renewable energy sources such as wind and solar. By diversifying their energy mix, Canada and Russia can ensure a stable and resilient energy grid that is less susceptible to fluctuations in weather conditions. The combination of these renewable energy sources can provide a comprehensive solution to meet the growing energy demands of both nations.

Furthermore, the development of hydroelectric power in the Arctic can foster international collaboration in research and technology exchange. Canada and Russia can share expertise and knowledge in dam construction, environmental impact assessments, and sustainable energy practices. This collaboration can lead to the development of best practices for hydroelectric power generation in the Arctic, benefiting not only these countries but also the global community.

In conclusion, hydroelectric power generation represents a significant opportunity for Canada and Russia in the post-global warming world. By utilizing the Arctic's abundant water resources, both nations can become leaders in renewable energy production, reduce their carbon footprint, and contribute to global efforts to combat climate change. It is imperative that politicians, educators, journalists, and the public recognize the potential of hydroelectric power generation in the Arctic and support its development as a key pillar of sustainable energy transition.

Chapter 4: Tourism and ecotourism

Arctic Tourism: Exploring the Potential for Growth in Canada and Russia

As global warming continues to reshape the Arctic landscape, Canada and Russia find themselves at the forefront of a new era of opportunity. The melting ice and increased accessibility of the region present numerous avenues for growth and development. In this subchapter, we will explore the potential for Arctic tourism in Canada and Russia, highlighting the economic, ecological, and cultural benefits it can bring.

With the effects of global warming becoming more evident, tourists from around the world are increasingly drawn to the Arctic regions to witness the unique environmental changes and wildlife. Canada and Russia, with their vast Arctic territories, have the potential to become leading destinations for Arctic tourism. From the breathtaking landscapes and diverse wildlife to the indigenous cultures and traditions, the Arctic offers a truly mesmerizing experience for visitors.

In addition to traditional tourism, there is also a growing interest in ecotourism, which focuses on sustainable and responsible travel. The Arctic's delicate ecosystem requires careful management to ensure its preservation and minimize the impact of tourism activities. By embracing ecotourism principles, Canada and Russia can attract environmentally conscious travelers who seek authentic experiences while contributing to the conservation of the Arctic environment.

Furthermore, the growth of tourism in the Arctic can have significant economic benefits for both countries. It can create employment opportunities, stimulate local businesses, and contribute to the overall economic development of remote Arctic communities. By investing in infrastructure and promoting tourism-related services, Canada and

Russia can maximize the positive impact of this industry on their economies.

Moreover, Arctic tourism can serve as a platform for cultural exchange and understanding. Indigenous communities in Canada and Russia have deep-rooted connections to the Arctic and possess invaluable traditional knowledge. By involving indigenous peoples in tourism activities and promoting cultural preservation, both countries can ensure the sustainability of their unique cultural heritage while fostering mutual respect and understanding among visitors.

It is important for politicians, educators, journalists, and the general public to recognize the potential of Arctic tourism in Canada and Russia. By supporting the development of this industry, we can capitalize on the post-global warming opportunities while safeguarding the delicate Arctic environment and empowering local communities. This subchapter aims to shed light on the possibilities that lie ahead and encourages all stakeholders to embrace Arctic tourism as a catalyst for sustainable growth, cultural preservation, and international cooperation.

Witnessing Environmental Changes: The Allure of Arctic Ecotourism

The Arctic region is undergoing rapid and unprecedented environmental changes due to global warming. As the effects of climate change become more evident, an increasing number of tourists are drawn to this unique and fragile ecosystem. In this subchapter, we explore the allure of Arctic ecotourism and the opportunities it presents for Canada and Russia.

Arctic resource extraction has become more accessible due to the melting ice, providing opportunities for increased mining, oil and gas extraction, and other resource-based industries. Both Canada and Russia can capitalize on these opportunities, leading to economic growth and job creation.

Moreover, the shift towards renewable energy sources offers immense potential for both countries. With their vast landscapes, Canada and Russia can harness wind, solar, and hydroelectric power, becoming leaders in clean energy production. This not only helps combat climate change but also creates a sustainable and resilient economy.

Tourism and ecotourism are emerging as significant industries in the Arctic. As the effects of global warming become more pronounced, tourists are eager to witness the unique environmental changes and wildlife in the region. Canada and Russia can leverage this growing interest by developing sustainable tourism practices, ensuring the protection of fragile ecosystems while providing visitors with an unforgettable experience.

The melting Arctic ice also brings new fishing grounds and opportunities for aquaculture. Canada and Russia can expand their fishing industries, meeting the growing global demand for seafood. By implementing responsible fishing practices, they can ensure the long-term sustainability of these industries.

The opening of new Arctic shipping routes presents an opportunity for infrastructure development. Canada and Russia can invest in ports and shipping lanes, facilitating increased trade and transportation between Europe and Asia. This not only enhances economic ties but also strengthens their geopolitical position.

The changing climate in the Arctic necessitates research and scientific collaboration. Canada and Russia can collaborate on initiatives focused on climate change, adaptation strategies, and environmental preservation. By sharing knowledge and resources, they can contribute to global efforts in combating climate change.

Both Canada and Russia can also take advantage of emerging carbon offset markets. By investing in carbon capture and storage technologies, offering carbon credits, and participating in emissions trading, they can contribute to global efforts in reducing greenhouse gas emissions.

As the effects of global warming become more pronounced, Canada and Russia can develop and export expertise in climate change adaptation and resilience planning. This expertise can benefit other nations facing similar challenges, leading to collaborations and economic opportunities.

Preserving indigenous land management practices and traditional knowledge is crucial in the face of climate change. Canada and Russia can support the preservation of indigenous cultures, fostering cultural diversity and sustainable land-use practices.

Lastly, as economic and geopolitical interests in the Arctic grow, Canada and Russia can play a significant role in shaping international agreements, regulations, and governance frameworks related to Arctic affairs. Their leadership can ensure the sustainable and responsible development of the region.

In conclusion, the allure of Arctic ecotourism is undeniable. By capitalizing on the opportunities presented by resource extraction, renewable energy, tourism, fisheries, infrastructure development, research collaboration, carbon offset markets, adaptation strategies, indigenous land management, and Arctic diplomacy, Canada and Russia can position themselves as the big winners in the post-global warming world.

Wildlife Tourism: Showcasing the Unique Arctic Fauna

Subchapter: Wildlife Tourism: Showcasing the Unique Arctic Fauna

As the effects of global warming continue to reshape the Arctic region, Canada and Russia have the opportunity to capitalize on the changing environment by attracting tourists interested in witnessing the unique wildlife and environmental changes in this pristine habitat. Wildlife tourism in the Arctic not only offers an extraordinary experience for visitors but also presents economic opportunities and helps raise awareness about the importance of preserving this fragile ecosystem.

The Arctic is home to a diverse range of fascinating species, including polar bears, walruses, seals, Arctic foxes, and numerous bird species. These iconic animals, adapted to survive in extreme cold and harsh conditions, have become the symbols of the Arctic and draw tourists from around the world.

Canada and Russia, with their expansive Arctic territories, are in a prime position to develop sustainable wildlife tourism initiatives. By establishing responsible guidelines and regulations, they can ensure that these activities do not harm the fragile ecosystems or disrupt the natural behavior of the wildlife.

Tourists interested in wildlife tourism in the Arctic can embark on guided tours, photography expeditions, and even participate in citizen science projects, where they contribute to ongoing research efforts. These experiences not only provide an up-close encounter with Arctic wildlife but also educate visitors about the importance of conservation and the need to protect these habitats.

In addition to showcasing the unique fauna, wildlife tourism in the Arctic can also create jobs and stimulate the local economies of Arctic communities. By investing in infrastructure development, such as eco-lodges, visitor centers, and transportation, Canada and Russia can support the growth of this industry and ensure a positive impact on local communities.

Furthermore, by promoting responsible wildlife tourism practices, Canada and Russia can establish themselves as leaders in sustainable ecotourism. This will attract environmentally conscious travelers, who are increasingly seeking responsible and authentic experiences.

The unique and fragile Arctic ecosystem is a valuable asset that needs protection, and wildlife tourism can play a significant role in raising awareness and generating support for conservation efforts. By showcasing the extraordinary wildlife and environmental changes in the Arctic, Canada and Russia can not only benefit economically but also contribute to the global understanding and preservation of this vital region.

Ultimately, wildlife tourism in the Arctic can be a win-win situation: it provides economic opportunities for Canada and Russia while promoting conservation and sustainable practices. By embracing this potential, these countries can establish themselves as leaders in the post-global warming world and demonstrate their commitment to environmental stewardship to politicians, educators, journalists, and the public.

Chapter 5: Fisheries and aquaculture

Shifting Fishing Grounds: Adapting to Changing Arctic Conditions

As global warming continues to transform the Arctic region, Canada and Russia are capitalizing on the post-global warming opportunities that arise. One area of significant potential lies in the shifting fishing grounds and the need to adapt to the changing conditions in order to maximize the benefits.

With the melting ice in the Arctic, new fishing grounds are emerging, offering immense opportunities for both Canada and Russia to expand their fishing industries. As traditional fishing grounds become less viable, there is a need to explore and exploit the untapped resources in these newly accessible areas. This shift presents an opportunity to meet the growing global demand for seafood and to generate economic growth and employment in the fishing sector.

In addition to traditional fishing, there is also potential for aquaculture in the Arctic region. The melting ice opens up possibilities for fish farming and other forms of aquaculture, allowing for the cultivation of various species in controlled environments. This presents an opportunity for Canada and Russia to further expand their aquaculture industries and diversify their seafood offerings.

However, adapting to the changing Arctic conditions requires careful planning and sustainable practices. Both Canada and Russia must prioritize the conservation of marine ecosystems and the protection of vulnerable species. This can be achieved through the implementation of responsible fishing practices, the establishment of protected areas, and the adoption of sustainable aquaculture methods.

Furthermore, collaboration between Canada and Russia in the realm of fisheries and aquaculture is essential. Sharing scientific knowledge and best practices can contribute to the development of sustainable fishing and aquaculture industries in the Arctic. This collaboration can also extend to the sharing of resources, technology, and expertise to ensure the long-term viability and resilience of these industries.

As politicians, educators, journalists, and the general public, it is important to recognize the opportunities and challenges associated with shifting fishing grounds in the Arctic. We must advocate for responsible fishing practices and sustainable aquaculture methods, while also supporting research and scientific collaboration in the field. By doing so, Canada and Russia can effectively adapt to changing Arctic conditions, maximize the economic benefits, and contribute to the global demand for seafood in an environmentally conscious manner.

Expanding Aquaculture: Seizing the Opportunity for Sustainable Seafood Production

The Arctic region is undergoing significant changes due to global warming, presenting unique opportunities for Canada and Russia. One such opportunity is the expansion of fisheries and aquaculture, which can meet the growing global demand for seafood while promoting sustainability and economic growth.

As the Arctic ice melts, new fishing grounds emerge, providing Canada and Russia with the chance to expand their fishing industries. With proper management and regulations in place, this expansion can be done sustainably, ensuring the long-term health and abundance of marine resources. By investing in modern fishing techniques and technologies, both countries can increase their seafood production and become major players in the global seafood market.

In addition to traditional fishing, aquaculture can play a crucial role in meeting the rising demand for seafood. The Arctic's pristine waters and cold temperatures provide an ideal environment for aquaculture operations. By cultivating fish, shellfish, and other marine organisms in controlled conditions, Canada and Russia can reduce the pressure on wild fish stocks while providing a reliable source of high-quality seafood.

However, it is essential to prioritize sustainability in aquaculture practices. By using environmentally friendly feed, minimizing waste, and monitoring water quality, Canada and Russia can ensure that their aquaculture operations have minimal impact on the fragile Arctic ecosystem. Additionally, investing in research and innovation can further improve the efficiency and sustainability of aquaculture practices.

Expanding aquaculture not only benefits the economy but also creates job opportunities, particularly in remote Arctic communities. It allows for the development of a skilled workforce and supports the growth of local businesses and infrastructure.

To seize the opportunity for sustainable seafood production, Canada and Russia must collaborate on research initiatives, share best practices, and establish effective governance frameworks. By working together, they can develop adaptive management strategies that ensure the long-term viability of their fisheries and aquaculture industries.

With the world's increasing demand for seafood and the changing climate in the Arctic, expanding aquaculture is a promising avenue for economic prosperity and environmental stewardship. Canada and Russia have the potential to become leaders in sustainable seafood production, contributing to food security, job creation, and the conservation of the Arctic's unique marine ecosystem. By seizing this opportunity, both countries can realize the full potential of the post-global warming world.

Meeting Global Demand: Canada and Russia's Role in the Seafood Industry

As global warming continues to impact the Arctic region, Canada and Russia are uniquely positioned to capitalize on the emerging opportunities in the seafood industry. The melting ice has opened up new fishing grounds and created favorable conditions for aquaculture, allowing both countries to expand their fishing industries and meet the growing global demand for seafood.

Canada and Russia possess vast coastlines and abundant marine resources, making them natural leaders in the seafood industry. The melting ice in the Arctic has resulted in the migration of fish species, creating new opportunities for fishing. Additionally, the warmer waters have facilitated the growth of aquaculture, providing a sustainable and controlled environment for seafood production.

Both countries can leverage their expertise and resources to develop sustainable fishing practices and ensure the long-term viability of the industry. By implementing responsible harvesting methods, such as quotas and conservation measures, Canada and Russia can maintain healthy fish populations and protect the delicate Arctic ecosystem.

Meeting the global demand for seafood presents a significant economic opportunity for Canada and Russia. The seafood industry is a vital source of income and employment for coastal communities, contributing to their economic growth and stability. By expanding their fishing industries, both countries can create new jobs and stimulate local economies.

Furthermore, as the effects of global warming become more pronounced, the demand for sustainable and responsibly sourced seafood is increasing. Canada and Russia can position themselves as leaders in this regard, catering to environmentally conscious consumers and capitalizing on the growing market for sustainable seafood products.

To fully realize the potential of the seafood industry, Canada and Russia should invest in research and development, innovation, and technology. By enhancing their capabilities in areas such as fish stock assessment, aquaculture techniques, and seafood processing, both countries can increase their competitiveness in the global market.

Collaboration between Canada and Russia in the seafood industry is also essential. By sharing knowledge, best practices, and scientific research, both countries can enhance their capabilities and ensure the sustainable management of resources. This collaboration can take the form of joint research initiatives, knowledge exchange programs, and industry partnerships.

In conclusion, the melting ice in the Arctic presents a unique opportunity for Canada and Russia to meet the growing global demand for seafood. By expanding their fishing industries and investing in sustainable practices, both countries can capitalize on this opportunity, create economic growth, and position themselves as leaders in the global seafood market. Collaboration, research, and responsible management will be key to ensuring the long-term viability and success of the seafood industry in the Arctic.

Chapter 6: Infrastructure development and shipping routes

The Opening of Arctic Shipping Routes: Implications for Canada and Russia

With the rapidly melting ice in the Arctic region, new shipping routes are becoming accessible, presenting significant opportunities and implications for both Canada and Russia. This subchapter explores the potential benefits and challenges that arise from the opening of these Arctic shipping routes.

Infrastructure development and shipping routes are crucial for facilitating increased trade and transportation between Europe and Asia. Canada and Russia can seize this opportunity by investing in the development of ports and shipping lanes. This investment will not only boost their economies but also position them as key players in global trade.

The accessibility of natural resources in the Arctic region due to melting ice is a game-changer for both Canada and Russia. Increased mining, oil and gas extraction, and other resource-based industries can flourish, providing immense economic benefits. Both countries can capitalize on this by effectively extracting and utilizing these resources to meet the growing global demand.

Furthermore, the shift towards renewable energy sources opens doors for Canada and Russia to become leaders in clean energy production. With their vast potential for wind, solar, and hydroelectric power generation, they can tap into these resources and contribute to a greener future.

As the effects of global warming become more evident, the Arctic regions become increasingly attractive to tourists interested in witnessing unique environmental changes and wildlife. Canada and Russia can leverage this opportunity to promote tourism and ecotourism, boosting their economies while raising awareness about the impacts of climate change.

The melting ice also creates new fishing grounds and opportunities for aquaculture. Both Canada and Russia can expand their fishing industries to meet the growing global demand for seafood. This not only stimulates economic growth but also promotes sustainable fishing practices.

Canada and Russia can collaborate on research initiatives focused on climate change, adaptation strategies, and environmental preservation. By pooling their resources and expertise, they can make significant contributions to scientific knowledge and find innovative solutions to the challenges posed by a changing climate.

Furthermore, both countries can take advantage of emerging carbon offset markets by investing in carbon capture and storage technologies, offering carbon credits, and participating in emissions trading. This not only helps combat climate change but also presents economic opportunities.

The effects of global warming necessitate the development of adaptation and resilience strategies. Canada and Russia can develop and export their expertise in climate change adaptation and resilience planning, supporting other nations facing similar challenges.

Preservation of indigenous land management practices and traditional knowledge is crucial in the face of climate change. Canada and Russia can support the preservation of these practices, fostering cultural preservation and sustainable land-use practices.

Finally, as economic and geopolitical interests in the Arctic region increase, Canada and Russia can play a significant role in shaping international agreements, regulations, and governance frameworks related to Arctic affairs. This allows them to safeguard their interests and ensure sustainable development in the region.

In conclusion, the opening of Arctic shipping routes presents numerous opportunities for Canada and Russia. From resource extraction to renewable energy development, from tourism to research collaboration, both countries stand to benefit greatly from the changing Arctic landscape. By effectively leveraging these opportunities, they can not only capitalize on post-global warming opportunities but also contribute to global efforts towards a sustainable future.

Investing in Arctic Infrastructure: Building Ports and Shipping Lanes

As the effects of global warming continue to reshape the Arctic region, Canada and Russia have emerged as frontrunners in capitalizing on the post-global warming opportunities. One area where both countries can make significant investments is in the development of Arctic infrastructure, specifically ports and shipping lanes.

With the melting of Arctic ice, new shipping routes have opened up, connecting Europe and Asia in a more efficient and cost-effective manner. Canada and Russia are strategically positioned to take advantage of these routes, as they offer the shortest distance between these two economic powerhouses. By investing in the construction and modernization of ports and shipping lanes, both countries can facilitate increased trade and transportation, bolstering their economies and strengthening their positions as global trade leaders.

The development of ports and shipping lanes in the Arctic region not only benefits Canada and Russia but also has positive implications for the global economy. The reduced shipping time and costs can lead to lower prices for goods, increased access to new markets, and enhanced trade relationships between nations. Additionally, the construction of these infrastructure projects creates jobs and stimulates economic growth, benefiting local communities and industries.

Moreover, investing in Arctic infrastructure aligns with the broader goals of sustainable development and environmental stewardship. By implementing state-of-the-art technologies and employing best practices in construction, both Canada and Russia can ensure that these projects minimize their environmental impact. They can also incorporate renewable energy sources into the infrastructure, further positioning themselves as leaders in clean energy production.

In addition to the economic and environmental benefits, the development of Arctic infrastructure presents an opportunity for Canada and Russia to strengthen their diplomatic ties and collaborate on governance frameworks. With increased economic and geopolitical interests in the Arctic, both countries can play a significant role in shaping international agreements and regulations related to Arctic affairs. By working together, they can foster cooperation, ensure sustainable development, and promote environmental preservation in the region.

Investing in Arctic infrastructure is not only an opportunity for economic growth and global trade but also a chance for Canada and Russia to establish themselves as leaders in sustainable development, environmental stewardship, and international cooperation. As politicians, educators, journalists, and the public, it is crucial to recognize and support these investments as they have the potential to bring immense benefits to both nations and the world at large.

Facilitating Trade and Transportation: Enhancing Connections between Europe and Asia

In the rapidly changing global landscape, the Arctic region is emerging as a key player, providing immense opportunities for Canada and Russia to capitalize on the post-global warming world. As politicians, educators, journalists, and the public, it is crucial to understand the potential benefits and challenges that lie ahead. One significant aspect to consider is the facilitation of trade and transportation, particularly the enhancement of connections between Europe and Asia.

With the melting ice in the Arctic, new shipping routes are opening up, presenting a game-changing opportunity for Canada and Russia. Both countries can seize this moment to invest in infrastructure development, such as ports and shipping lanes, to create efficient and reliable trade routes. This would not only boost economic growth but also foster stronger ties between Europe and Asia, bringing nations closer together.

Furthermore, as the demand for natural resources continues to rise, the Arctic's accessibility becomes a significant advantage for Canada and Russia. The increased mining, oil and gas extraction, and other resource-based industries can fuel economic growth and create employment opportunities. By focusing on sustainable practices, both countries can ensure responsible resource extraction, balancing economic growth with environmental preservation.

Renewable energy development is another avenue that holds great potential for Canada and Russia. With their vast landscapes and untapped resources, both countries can become leaders in clean energy production. Wind, solar, and hydroelectric power generation can provide sustainable alternatives, reducing dependence on fossil fuels and mitigating climate change.

The unique environmental changes and wildlife in the Arctic regions make it a prime destination for tourists. Canada and Russia can leverage this opportunity by promoting tourism and ecotourism. By showcasing the breathtaking landscapes and the effects of global warming, both countries can attract tourists who are eager to experience these changes firsthand, contributing to local economies and raising awareness about the importance of environmental conservation.

As the Arctic ice melts, new fishing grounds and opportunities for aquaculture arise. Canada and Russia can expand their fishing industries and meet the growing global demand for seafood. By implementing sustainable fishing practices, both countries can ensure the long-term viability of these industries while supporting local communities.

Collaboration and research initiatives focused on climate change are crucial in understanding and adapting to the changing Arctic climate. Canada and Russia can join forces to study climate change, develop adaptation strategies, and preserve the delicate Arctic ecosystem. This scientific collaboration will not only benefit the two countries but also contribute to international efforts to combat climate change.

The emerging carbon offset markets offer an avenue for both Canada and Russia to participate in emissions trading and invest in carbon capture and storage technologies. By leading the way in carbon reduction efforts, both countries can position themselves as leaders in environmental stewardship and attract green investments.

With the effects of global warming becoming more pronounced, Canada and Russia can develop and export expertise in climate change adaptation and resilience planning. By assisting other nations facing similar challenges, both countries can create a sustainable future for all.

Preserving indigenous land management practices and traditional knowledge is of paramount importance in the face of climate change. Canada and Russia can support indigenous communities and their sustainable land-use practices, fostering cultural preservation and creating a harmonious relationship between humans and the environment.

Lastly, as economic and geopolitical interests grow in the Arctic region, Canada and Russia can play a significant role in shaping international agreements, regulations, and governance frameworks. By actively engaging in Arctic diplomacy, both countries can ensure that the region's resources are managed sustainably and that the interests of all stakeholders are considered.

In conclusion, the facilitation of trade and transportation between Europe and Asia in the post-global warming world presents immense opportunities for Canada and Russia. By investing in infrastructure development, focusing on sustainable practices, promoting renewable energy, attracting tourists, expanding fishing industries, fostering research collaborations, participating in carbon offset markets, developing adaptation strategies, preserving indigenous knowledge, and engaging in Arctic diplomacy, both countries can emerge as the big winners in the new Arctic era.

Chapter 7: Research and scientific collaboration

The Importance of Arctic Research: Collaborative Efforts by Canada and Russia

In a rapidly changing world, the Arctic region stands at the forefront of global attention. As the effects of global warming become increasingly evident, Canada and Russia find themselves in a unique position to capitalize on the opportunities presented by this new reality. Through collaborative efforts in Arctic research, both nations can not only benefit economically but also contribute to the preservation and sustainable development of this fragile ecosystem.

Arctic resource extraction has become a key focus for Canada and Russia. With the melting ice opening up previously inaccessible areas, both countries can tap into the vast natural resources found in the region. Increased mining, oil and gas extraction, and other resource-based industries offer immense economic potential. However, it is crucial that these activities are carried out responsibly and with a strong emphasis on environmental protection.

The shift towards renewable energy sources presents another avenue for Canada and Russia to capitalize on post-global warming opportunities. With their vast potential for wind, solar, and hydroelectric power generation, both countries can become leaders in clean energy production. By investing in renewable energy development, they can not only reduce their reliance on fossil fuels but also export clean energy solutions to other nations.

Tourism and ecotourism also hold promise for Canada and Russia. As the Arctic landscape undergoes rapid changes, tourists are increasingly drawn to witness the unique environmental transformations and wildlife in the region. By promoting sustainable tourism practices, both countries can attract visitors while also ensuring the preservation of the Arctic's delicate ecosystem.

The melting of the Arctic ice presents new possibilities in the realm of fisheries and aquaculture. With new fishing grounds emerging and the potential for aquaculture, Canada and Russia can expand their fishing industries to meet the growing global demand for seafood. It is essential, however, that sustainable fishing practices are implemented to protect the delicate balance of marine ecosystems.

The opening of new Arctic shipping routes offers significant opportunities for infrastructure development. Canada and Russia can invest in ports and shipping lanes to facilitate increased trade and transportation between Europe and Asia. This will not only boost economic growth but also strengthen geopolitical ties and foster cooperation between nations.

Research and scientific collaboration are of paramount importance in understanding and mitigating the effects of climate change in the Arctic. Canada and Russia have the opportunity to collaborate on research initiatives focused on climate change, adaptation strategies, and environmental preservation. By sharing knowledge and resources, they can contribute to the global effort to combat climate change and ensure the sustainability of the Arctic ecosystem.

Carbon offset markets and emissions trading are emerging as key mechanisms to reduce greenhouse gas emissions. Both Canada and Russia can take advantage of these markets by investing in carbon capture and storage technologies, offering carbon credits, and participating in emissions trading. This not only supports the transition to a low-carbon economy but also presents economic opportunities for both countries.

As the effects of global warming become more pronounced, Canada and Russia can develop and export expertise in climate change adaptation and resilience planning. By sharing their knowledge and experiences, they can assist other nations facing similar challenges and contribute to global efforts in adapting to a changing climate.

Preserving indigenous land management practices and traditional knowledge is crucial in the face of climate change. Canada and Russia can support indigenous communities in preserving their cultural heritage and sustainable land-use practices. By incorporating traditional knowledge into their policies and practices, they can foster cultural preservation while ensuring the sustainable development of the Arctic region.

Finally, as economic and geopolitical interests in the Arctic region grow, Canada and Russia have the opportunity to play a significant role in shaping international agreements, regulations, and governance frameworks. Through Arctic diplomacy and governance, they can advocate for sustainable practices, environmental protection, and the equitable sharing of resources.

In conclusion, collaborative efforts in Arctic research between Canada and Russia are of paramount importance. The economic opportunities presented by the post-global warming world must be balanced with the need for environmental preservation and sustainable development. By harnessing their vast resources, investing in renewable energy, promoting responsible tourism, and supporting scientific research, Canada and Russia can become leaders in the Arctic region while setting a precedent for global cooperation and environmental stewardship.

Climate Change Studies: Understanding the Arctic's Role in Global Climate Patterns

As the effects of global warming continue to reshape the world, understanding the Arctic's role in global climate patterns is crucial. The Arctic region is experiencing some of the most rapid and profound changes due to rising temperatures, and Canada and Russia are at the forefront of these transformations. In this subchapter, we will explore the various opportunities and challenges that arise from these changes, addressing a diverse audience of politicians, educators, journalists, and the public.

Arctic resource extraction is one major opportunity that both Canada and Russia can capitalize on. The melting ice in the region has made natural resources more accessible, paving the way for increased mining, oil and gas extraction, and other resource-based industries. This presents economic benefits for both countries, but also raises concerns regarding environmental impacts and sustainable practices.

Another avenue for growth lies in renewable energy development. With their vast territories, Canada and Russia have significant potential for wind, solar, and hydroelectric power generation. By investing in clean energy, both countries can become leaders in sustainable energy production, reducing their reliance on fossil fuels and mitigating the impacts of climate change.

The changing Arctic landscape also offers opportunities for tourism and ecotourism. As global warming alters the environment and wildlife in the region, Canada and Russia can attract tourists interested in witnessing these unique changes firsthand. This not only drives economic growth but also raises awareness about the importance of preserving these delicate ecosystems.

Moreover, the melting Arctic ice opens up new fishing grounds and opportunities for aquaculture. Canada and Russia can expand their fishing industries to meet the growing global demand for seafood, while ensuring sustainable practices to protect marine life and preserve the balance of the Arctic ecosystem.

Infrastructure development and shipping routes are also key considerations in the post-global warming world. As new Arctic shipping routes open up, Canada and Russia can invest in infrastructure such as ports and shipping lanes, facilitating increased trade and transportation between Europe and Asia. This presents economic benefits but also raises concerns about the potential environmental impacts of increased shipping activity.

The changing Arctic climate also calls for increased research and scientific collaboration. Canada and Russia can work together on research initiatives focused on climate change, adaptation strategies, and environmental preservation. By sharing knowledge and resources, they can make significant contributions to our understanding of the Arctic's role in global climate patterns.

Furthermore, both countries can take advantage of emerging carbon offset markets and emissions trading. By investing in carbon capture and storage technologies and offering carbon credits, Canada and Russia can participate in the fight against climate change while benefiting economically.

As the effects of global warming become more pronounced, Canada and Russia can develop and export expertise in climate change adaptation and resilience planning. By sharing their knowledge and experiences, they can help other nations facing similar challenges to develop effective strategies to mitigate the impacts of climate change.

Preserving indigenous land management practices and traditional knowledge is another crucial aspect of climate change adaptation. Canada and Russia can support indigenous communities in preserving their cultural practices and sustainable land-use practices, fostering both cultural preservation and environmental sustainability.

Lastly, the economic and geopolitical interests in the Arctic region provide an opportunity for Canada and Russia to play a significant role in shaping international agreements, regulations, and governance frameworks. By engaging in Arctic diplomacy and governance, both countries can contribute to the sustainable and responsible management of this critical region.

In conclusion, understanding the Arctic's role in global climate patterns is essential for policymakers, educators, journalists, and the public. Canada and Russia have the potential to benefit from increased economic opportunities in the post-global warming world, ranging from resource extraction and renewable energy development to tourism and scientific collaboration. However, it is crucial to approach these opportunities with a focus on sustainability, environmental preservation, and respect for indigenous communities and their traditional knowledge. By doing so, Canada and Russia can become leaders in addressing the challenges and opportunities presented by climate change in the Arctic.

Adaptation Strategies: Developing Resilience in the Face of Changing Arctic Conditions

As the Arctic region undergoes rapid changes due to global warming, Canada and Russia are poised to reap the benefits and capitalize on the emerging opportunities. This subchapter explores the various adaptation strategies that both nations can employ to develop resilience and thrive in the post-global warming world.

Arctic resource extraction offers immense potential for Canada and Russia. With the melting ice opening up previously inaccessible areas, mining, oil and gas extraction, and other resource-based industries can experience a significant boom. Both nations can harness these opportunities and become leaders in resource extraction, bolstering their economies and creating employment opportunities.

The shift towards renewable energy sources presents another avenue for growth. Canada and Russia possess vast potential for wind, solar, and hydroelectric power generation. By investing in renewable energy development, both countries can position themselves as pioneers in clean energy production, reducing their reliance on fossil fuels and contributing to global efforts to combat climate change.

The changing Arctic landscape also provides a unique opportunity for tourism and ecotourism. As the effects of global warming become more evident, tourists from around the world will be drawn to witness the remarkable environmental changes and diverse wildlife in the Arctic regions. By promoting sustainable tourism practices, Canada and Russia can attract visitors while preserving the fragile Arctic ecosystem.

The melting ice in the Arctic also opens up new fishing grounds and opportunities for aquaculture. Canada and Russia can expand their fishing industries, meeting the growing global demand for seafood. By implementing responsible fishing practices and sustainable aquaculture methods, both nations can ensure the long-term viability of these industries.

In order to facilitate increased trade and transportation between Europe and Asia, Canada and Russia can invest in infrastructure development. The opening of new Arctic shipping routes necessitates the construction of ports and shipping lanes. This investment not only enhances economic opportunities but also strengthens geopolitical influence.

The changing climate in the Arctic calls for research and scientific collaboration. Canada and Russia can collaborate on research initiatives focused on climate change, adaptation strategies, and environmental preservation. By sharing knowledge and expertise, both nations can contribute to global efforts in understanding and mitigating the impacts of climate change.

Taking advantage of emerging carbon offset markets is another avenue for Canada and Russia to explore. By investing in carbon capture and storage technologies, offering carbon credits, and participating in emissions trading, both countries can play a pivotal role in reducing greenhouse gas emissions and combatting climate change.

Canada and Russia can also develop and export their expertise in climate change adaptation and resilience planning. As the effects of global warming become more pronounced, other nations facing similar challenges will seek guidance in adapting to changing conditions. By sharing their knowledge and experience, Canada and Russia can establish themselves as leaders in climate change adaptation strategies.

Preserving indigenous land management practices and traditional knowledge is essential in the face of climate change. Canada and Russia can support indigenous communities in maintaining their sustainable land-use practices, fostering cultural preservation, and ensuring the long-term sustainability of the Arctic ecosystem.

Finally, with increased economic and geopolitical interests in the Arctic region, Canada and Russia have the opportunity to shape international agreements, regulations, and governance frameworks. By actively engaging in Arctic diplomacy, both nations can play a significant role in ensuring the sustainable development and environmental protection of this unique region.

In conclusion, Canada and Russia are well-positioned to thrive in the post-global warming world by implementing adaptation strategies that promote resilience and capitalize on emerging opportunities. From resource extraction to renewable energy development, tourism to scientific collaboration, both nations can lead the way in sustainable development and contribute to global efforts in mitigating climate change.

Chapter 8: Carbon offset markets and emissions trading

The Emergence of Carbon Offset Markets: Opportunities for Canada and Russia

As the global community grapples with the urgent need to address climate change, the emergence of carbon offset markets presents a significant opportunity for both Canada and Russia. These markets provide a mechanism for countries to reduce their greenhouse gas emissions by investing in projects that offset their carbon footprint. This subchapter explores the potential benefits and opportunities that carbon offset markets can bring to Canada and Russia.

Both Canada and Russia have vast territories and abundant natural resources, making them well-positioned to capitalize on carbon offset markets. By investing in carbon capture and storage technologies, these nations can reduce their own emissions and offer carbon credits to other countries. This not only helps mitigate the effects of climate change but also generates economic benefits through the sale of carbon credits.

Furthermore, participation in carbon offset markets can spur innovation and investment in renewable energy development. Canada and Russia can tap into their vast potential for wind, solar, and hydroelectric power generation, becoming leaders in clean energy production. This not only helps reduce reliance on fossil fuels but also creates new jobs and economic opportunities in the renewable energy sector.

In addition to renewable energy, carbon offset markets can also benefit other industries in the Arctic region. With the melting ice opening up new shipping routes, Canada and Russia can invest in infrastructure development, such as ports and shipping lanes, to facilitate increased trade and transportation between Europe and Asia. This not only boosts economic growth but also reduces the carbon emissions associated with longer shipping routes.

The effects of global warming are also creating unique opportunities for tourism and ecotourism in the Arctic regions. As the environment changes, tourists are increasingly interested in witnessing these changes firsthand. Canada and Russia can capitalize on this by promoting their unique environmental changes and wildlife, attracting tourists and boosting local economies.

Furthermore, the changing climate in the Arctic presents an opportunity for Canada and Russia to collaborate on research initiatives focused on climate change, adaptation strategies, and environmental preservation. By working together, these nations can develop innovative solutions to address the challenges posed by climate change and share their expertise with the rest of the world.

In conclusion, the emergence of carbon offset markets offers numerous opportunities for Canada and Russia in the post-global warming world. From renewable energy development to tourism, fisheries, and research collaboration, these nations can capitalize on their unique resources and expertise to not only mitigate the effects of climate change but also drive economic growth and innovation. By embracing these opportunities, Canada and Russia can position themselves as leaders in the transition to a sustainable and resilient future.

Carbon Capture and Storage: Investing in Technologies for Emissions Reduction

In the face of global warming, nations around the world are seeking ways to reduce greenhouse gas emissions and combat climate change. Canada and Russia, as major players in the Arctic region, have a unique opportunity to invest in carbon capture and storage technologies, leading the way in emissions reduction efforts.

Carbon capture and storage (CCS) is a process that involves capturing carbon dioxide emissions from industrial sources, such as power plants and factories, and storing them underground or utilizing them for other purposes. This technology has the potential to significantly reduce carbon dioxide emissions and mitigate the impacts of climate change.

By investing in CCS technologies, both Canada and Russia can not only contribute to global emissions reduction efforts but also position themselves as leaders in sustainable development. This subchapter explores the various benefits and opportunities associated with carbon capture and storage in the context of a post-global warming world.

One of the key advantages of investing in CCS is the potential for economic growth and job creation. The development and deployment of CCS technologies require skilled labor and expertise, offering new employment opportunities in research, engineering, and project management. Moreover, the establishment of a CCS industry can attract investments and stimulate economic growth in related sectors.

Furthermore, CCS can provide a viable solution for industries heavily reliant on fossil fuels, such as mining, oil and gas extraction, and other resource-based industries. By implementing CCS technologies, these sectors can continue to operate while significantly reducing their carbon emissions, ensuring a sustainable and environmentally friendly future.

In addition to the economic benefits, investing in CCS technologies can also contribute to international climate commitments. Both Canada and Russia can participate in emissions trading and offer carbon credits through their CCS projects, promoting a global transition to a low-carbon economy.

Moreover, CCS can play a crucial role in achieving long-term emissions reduction targets. While renewable energy sources are essential for decarbonizing the energy sector, certain industries and processes may still rely on fossil fuels. CCS can provide a bridging solution by capturing and storing the carbon emissions from these sectors until cleaner alternatives are available.

Lastly, the development of CCS technologies aligns with the goals of the Paris Agreement and demonstrates a commitment to responsible environmental stewardship. By investing in emissions reduction technologies, both Canada and Russia can enhance their international reputation as leaders in sustainability and climate action.

In conclusion, carbon capture and storage technologies present significant opportunities for Canada and Russia in a post-global warming world. By investing in CCS, these nations can contribute to emissions reduction efforts, stimulate economic growth, and position themselves as leaders in sustainable development. It is crucial for policymakers, educators, journalists, and the public to recognize the potential of CCS and advocate for its implementation as part of a comprehensive climate change mitigation strategy.

Offering Carbon Credits: Leveraging Carbon Offset Initiatives

In the rapidly changing world affected by global warming, Canada and Russia have emerged as the big winners in the post-global warming era. As politicians, educators, journalists, and the public, it is crucial to understand the potential opportunities and challenges that lie ahead. One of the key strategies that both countries can leverage is offering carbon credits through carbon offset initiatives.

With the emergence of carbon offset markets and emissions trading, Canada and Russia have the opportunity to make significant strides in mitigating the effects of climate change. By investing in carbon capture and storage technologies, both countries can reduce their carbon emissions and offer carbon credits to other nations and industries seeking to offset their own emissions.

Participating in emissions trading not only reduces greenhouse gas emissions but also generates economic benefits. By selling carbon credits, Canada and Russia can generate revenue that can be reinvested in sustainable development projects, renewable energy initiatives, and other climate change mitigation efforts.

Furthermore, offering carbon credits can help both countries in their pursuit of sustainable development. By actively participating in carbon offset initiatives, Canada and Russia can showcase their commitment to environmental stewardship and attract international investments and partnerships. This can drive innovation in renewable energy development, infrastructure, and research initiatives focused on climate change adaptation strategies.

Additionally, by offering carbon credits, Canada and Russia can contribute to the preservation of fragile ecosystems in the Arctic region. These credits can be used to support indigenous land management practices and traditional knowledge, fostering cultural preservation and sustainable land-use practices. This approach aligns with the principles of sustainability and ensures that the unique environmental changes and wildlife in the Arctic regions are protected for future generations.

Moreover, by actively engaging in carbon offset initiatives, Canada and Russia can play a significant role in shaping international agreements, regulations, and governance frameworks related to Arctic affairs. Their leadership in this area can strengthen Arctic diplomacy and governance while promoting responsible resource extraction, tourism, and fisheries management practices.

In conclusion, offering carbon credits through carbon offset initiatives presents a crucial opportunity for Canada and Russia in the post-global warming world. It allows both countries to contribute to climate change mitigation efforts, attract investments, foster sustainable development, preserve indigenous knowledge, and play a significant role in shaping

Arctic governance. By leveraging carbon offset initiatives, Canada and Russia can position themselves as leaders in the transition to a low-carbon and sustainable future.

Emissions Trading: Participating in Global Efforts to Mitigate Climate Change

As the world grapples with the pressing issue of climate change, it is essential for nations like Canada and Russia to actively participate in global efforts to mitigate its impacts. One such avenue that holds immense potential is emissions trading. This subchapter explores how both countries can capitalize on this opportunity to address climate change and forge a sustainable future.

Emissions trading, also known as cap-and-trade, is an innovative market-based approach that allows countries to limit their greenhouse gas emissions while providing economic incentives for industries to reduce their carbon footprint. By participating in emissions trading, Canada and Russia can not only contribute to global emission reduction goals but also unlock numerous economic and environmental benefits.

Both Canada and Russia possess vast natural resources and industries that can play a pivotal role in emissions trading. Through the adoption of carbon capture and storage technologies, these nations can reduce their emissions and offer carbon credits in the emerging carbon offset markets. This presents an excellent opportunity to attract investment, create jobs, and stimulate economic growth while advancing climate change mitigation efforts.

Furthermore, active participation in emissions trading can foster international collaboration and scientific research. Canada and Russia can collaborate on research initiatives focused on climate change, adaptation strategies, and environmental preservation. By sharing knowledge and expertise, these nations can take a leading role in shaping global climate action and influencing international agreements and regulations.

Emissions trading also aligns with other post-global warming opportunities for Canada and Russia. The shift towards renewable energy sources presents a chance for both countries to tap into their vast potential for wind, solar, and hydroelectric power generation. By becoming leaders in clean energy production, they can not only reduce emissions but also strengthen their economies and create sustainable jobs.

Additionally, as the Arctic ice melts, new shipping routes emerge, opening doors for increased trade and transportation. Canada and Russia can invest in infrastructure development, such as ports and shipping lanes, to facilitate this growth. This will not only boost their economies but also enable efficient and environmentally friendly transportation, further contributing to climate change mitigation efforts.

In conclusion, emissions trading offers a significant opportunity for Canada and Russia to actively participate in global efforts to mitigate climate change. By investing in carbon capture technologies, offering carbon credits, and participating in emissions trading, these nations can simultaneously address environmental concerns and stimulate economic growth. Moreover, their active involvement in emissions trading can foster scientific collaboration, shape international agreements, and position them as leaders in climate change mitigation strategies. It is imperative for politicians, educators, journalists, and the general public to recognize and support these endeavors for a sustainable future.

Chapter 9: Adaptation and resilience strategies

Navigating the Effects of Global Warming: Developing Adaptation Strategies in Canada and Russia

In the book "The Arctic Boom: How Canada and Russia are Capitalizing on Post-Global Warming Opportunities," we explore the potential benefits and challenges that Canada and Russia face in a post-global warming world. This subchapter focuses on the development of adaptation strategies to navigate the effects of global warming in these two countries. It aims to address politicians, educators, journalists, the public, and individuals interested in the niches of Canada and Russia's opportunities in the post-global warming world.

Canada and Russia are poised to be the big winners in the post-global warming world due to their Arctic territories and the increased accessibility of natural resources. The melting ice in the Arctic region opens up new possibilities for resource extraction, including mining, oil and gas extraction, and other resource-based industries. Both countries can capitalize on this by investing in infrastructure, technology, and expertise to ensure sustainable and responsible resource extraction practices.

Furthermore, the shift towards renewable energy sources presents an excellent opportunity for both Canada and Russia to become leaders in clean energy production. With their vast potential for wind, solar, and hydroelectric power generation, they can develop and expand renewable energy projects, contributing to a greener future.

As the effects of global warming become more evident, Canada and Russia can leverage their unique environmental changes and wildlife in the Arctic regions to attract tourists. Tourism and ecotourism can provide a significant boost to the economy while raising awareness about the impacts of climate change.

The melting Arctic ice also brings new fishing grounds and aquaculture opportunities. Canada and Russia can expand their fishing industries to meet the growing global demand for seafood, ensuring sustainable practices are in place to protect the fragile Arctic ecosystem.

Additionally, the opening of new Arctic shipping routes presents an opportunity for both countries to invest in infrastructure development. Ports and shipping lanes can facilitate increased trade and transportation between Europe and Asia, positioning Canada and Russia as key players in global commerce.

Collaboration on research initiatives focused on climate change, adaptation strategies, and environmental preservation is another area of opportunity. By sharing knowledge and resources, Canada and Russia can make significant contributions to understanding and mitigating the effects of global warming.

Both countries can also take advantage of emerging carbon offset markets and emissions trading. Investing in carbon capture and storage technologies, offering carbon credits, and participating in emissions trading can contribute to global efforts to reduce greenhouse gas emissions.

As the effects of global warming become more pronounced, Canada and Russia can develop and export their expertise in climate change adaptation and resilience planning. This can help other nations facing similar challenges to navigate the impacts of global warming effectively.

Furthermore, supporting the preservation of indigenous land management practices and traditional knowledge is crucial. Canada and Russia can work towards fostering cultural preservation and sustainable land-use practices by involving indigenous communities in climate change adaptation strategies.

Finally, with their economic and geopolitical interests in the Arctic region, Canada and Russia can play a significant role in shaping international agreements, regulations, and governance frameworks related to Arctic affairs. By actively engaging in Arctic diplomacy, both countries can ensure that the region's resources and ecosystems are protected for future generations.

In conclusion, navigating the effects of global warming requires the development of adaptation strategies in Canada and Russia. These strategies encompass various sectors, including resource extraction, renewable energy, tourism, fisheries, infrastructure, research, carbon offset markets, adaptation and resilience, indigenous land management, and Arctic diplomacy. By capitalizing on post-global warming opportunities, Canada and Russia can position themselves as leaders in sustainable development and contribute to addressing the challenges of climate change on a global scale.

Exporting Expertise: Sharing Climate Change Adaptation and Resilience Planning with Other Nations

As the effects of global warming continue to reshape the Arctic region, Canada and Russia find themselves in a unique position to capitalize on the opportunities that arise in a post-global warming world. However, their success goes beyond resource extraction and economic gains. Both countries have the potential to become leaders in addressing climate change and sharing their expertise in climate change adaptation and resilience planning with other nations.

With the increasing accessibility of natural resources in the Arctic region due to melting ice, Canada and Russia stand to benefit from expanded mining, oil and gas extraction, and other resource-based industries.

However, they can also play a crucial role in promoting sustainable practices and responsible resource management. By implementing stringent environmental regulations, investing in clean technologies, and sharing best practices with other nations, Canada and Russia can ensure that resource extraction in the Arctic is done in an environmentally responsible manner.

In addition to resource extraction, both countries can tap into their vast potential for renewable energy development. With ample wind, solar, and hydroelectric power resources, Canada and Russia can become leaders in clean energy production. By investing in renewable energy infrastructure, promoting research and development, and fostering international collaborations, they can contribute to reducing global greenhouse gas emissions and combat climate change on a global scale.

The unique environmental changes and wildlife in the Arctic regions can also be a draw for tourists interested in witnessing the effects of global warming firsthand. Canada and Russia can capitalize on this by promoting tourism and ecotourism in the Arctic. By ensuring sustainable tourism practices and creating protected areas, they can showcase the beauty of the Arctic while also raising awareness about the impacts of climate change.

As the Arctic ice continues to melt, new fishing grounds and opportunities for aquaculture emerge. Canada and Russia can expand their fishing industries and meet the growing global demand for seafood. However, they must also prioritize sustainable fishing practices and protect vulnerable species to ensure the long-term viability of their fisheries.

The opening of new Arctic shipping routes presents an opportunity for Canada and Russia to invest in infrastructure development. By building ports and shipping lanes, they can facilitate increased trade and transportation between Europe and Asia, unlocking new economic opportunities. At the same time, they must ensure that these developments are done sustainably and do not harm the fragile Arctic ecosystem.

The changing climate in the Arctic also calls for increased research and scientific collaboration. Canada and Russia can lead the way by partnering on research initiatives focused on climate change, adaptation strategies, and environmental preservation. By sharing data, knowledge, and expertise, they can contribute to a better understanding of the impacts of global warming and develop effective solutions.

Both Canada and Russia can take advantage of the emerging carbon offset markets by investing in carbon capture and storage technologies and participating in emissions trading. By offering carbon credits and reducing their own emissions, they can contribute to global efforts to mitigate climate change.

As the effects of global warming become more pronounced, Canada and Russia can develop and export expertise in climate change adaptation and resilience planning to other nations facing similar challenges. By sharing their experiences, best practices, and innovative solutions, they can help other countries navigate the complexities of climate change and build resilience in the face of uncertainty.

Furthermore, Canada and Russia can support the preservation of indigenous land management practices and traditional knowledge in the face of climate change. By incorporating indigenous perspectives and knowledge into their climate change adaptation strategies, they can foster cultural preservation and promote sustainable land-use practices.

Lastly, with increased economic and geopolitical interests in the Arctic region, Canada and Russia can play a significant role in shaping international agreements, regulations, and governance frameworks related to Arctic affairs. By engaging in Arctic diplomacy and actively participating in international forums, they can ensure that the Arctic is managed sustainably and that the interests of all stakeholders are taken into account.

In conclusion, Canada and Russia have the potential to be the big winners in the post-global warming world. Beyond economic gains, they can lead the way in addressing climate change, promoting sustainable practices, and sharing their expertise with other nations. By focusing on areas such as renewable energy development, tourism, research collaboration, and indigenous land management, they can contribute to a more sustainable and resilient future for all.

Building Sustainable Futures: Promoting Resilience in Arctic Communities

As the effects of global warming continue to reshape the Arctic region, it is crucial for nations like Canada and Russia to consider the long-term sustainability and resilience of Arctic communities. In this subchapter, we will explore the various opportunities and challenges that both countries face in building sustainable futures for these communities.

Arctic resource extraction has become increasingly accessible due to melting ice, presenting Canada and Russia with the opportunity to capitalize on the abundance of natural resources in the region. With careful planning and responsible practices, increased mining, oil and gas extraction, and other resource-based industries can provide economic growth and stability for Arctic communities.

Furthermore, the shift towards renewable energy sources offers great potential for both Canada and Russia to become leaders in clean energy production. Wind, solar, and hydroelectric power generation can not only reduce reliance on fossil fuels but also provide employment opportunities and stimulate economic growth in Arctic communities.

The unique environmental changes and wildlife in the Arctic regions can attract tourists interested in witnessing the effects of global warming. Canada and Russia can develop sustainable tourism and ecotourism initiatives, promoting environmental preservation and the cultural richness of Arctic communities.

The melting Arctic ice opens up new fishing grounds and opportunities for aquaculture, allowing Canada and Russia to expand their fishing industries and meet the growing global demand for seafood. By implementing sustainable fishing practices, both countries can ensure the long-term viability of their fisheries.

The opening of new Arctic shipping routes presents an opportunity for Canada and Russia to invest in infrastructure development, such as ports and shipping lanes. This will facilitate increased trade and transportation between Europe and Asia, benefiting Arctic communities and the global economy.

Collaboration on research initiatives focused on climate change, adaptation strategies, and environmental preservation can strengthen the scientific capabilities of both Canada and Russia. By sharing knowledge and resources, these countries can make significant contributions to addressing the challenges posed by global warming.

Participating in carbon offset markets and emissions trading can provide economic incentives for both Canada and Russia to invest in carbon capture and storage technologies. By offering carbon credits and reducing emissions, these countries can contribute to mitigating the effects of climate change.

Canada and Russia can also develop and export expertise in climate change adaptation and resilience planning to other nations facing similar challenges. By sharing best practices and supporting sustainable development, these countries can foster global resilience in the face of a changing climate.

Lastly, it is essential for Canada and Russia to support the preservation of indigenous land management practices and traditional knowledge. By valuing and incorporating indigenous perspectives, these countries can ensure sustainable land-use practices and cultural preservation in the Arctic.

With their economic and geopolitical interests in the Arctic region, Canada and Russia can play a significant role in shaping international agreements, regulations, and governance frameworks related to Arctic affairs. By prioritizing sustainable development and resilience, both countries can contribute to the long-term well-being of Arctic communities and the preservation of this unique and fragile ecosystem.

In conclusion, building sustainable futures and promoting resilience in Arctic communities require a comprehensive approach that considers economic, environmental, and social factors. By capitalizing on opportunities such as resource extraction, renewable energy, tourism, fisheries, infrastructure development, research collaboration, carbon offset markets, adaptation strategies, indigenous land management, and diplomacy, Canada and Russia can lead the way in creating a sustainable and resilient Arctic for generations to come.

Chapter 10: Indigenous land management and traditional knowledge preservation

Indigenous Communities and Climate Change: Supporting Land Management Practices and Traditional Knowledge

In the face of the rapidly changing climate, it is essential to recognize and support the vital role that Indigenous communities play in land management practices and the preservation of traditional knowledge. Canada and Russia, as two of the major players in the post-global warming world, have a unique opportunity to champion the cause of Indigenous communities and create a sustainable future for the Arctic region.

Indigenous communities have been living in harmony with the land for centuries, possessing a deep understanding of the local ecosystems and the impacts of climate change. By supporting and incorporating their traditional knowledge into land management practices, Canada and Russia can ensure the preservation of cultural heritage and promote sustainable land-use practices.

These communities can provide valuable insights into adapting to the changing environment and developing resilience strategies. Their knowledge of traditional farming techniques, sustainable hunting and fishing practices, and natural resource management can contribute significantly to mitigating the effects of climate change.

Furthermore, by involving Indigenous communities in research initiatives focused on climate change, adaptation strategies, and environmental preservation, Canada and Russia can foster scientific collaboration and enhance our understanding of the Arctic region. This collaboration can lead to innovative solutions and inform policy decisions on climate change at national and international levels.

Moreover, by supporting Indigenous land management practices, Canada and Russia can promote sustainable economic development in the Arctic region. The conservation of biodiversity, responsible resource extraction, and the preservation of traditional livelihoods can attract tourists interested in witnessing the unique environmental changes and wildlife in the Arctic regions. This, in turn, can boost the tourism and ecotourism industries, benefiting the local economies.

In addition, Canada and Russia can play a significant role in shaping international agreements, regulations, and governance frameworks related to Arctic affairs. By advocating for the inclusion of Indigenous perspectives and rights, both countries can ensure that the interests and voices of Indigenous communities are represented and respected.

In conclusion, supporting Indigenous land management practices and traditional knowledge preservation is crucial for the sustainable development of the Arctic region in the face of climate change. Canada and Russia, as major players in the post-global warming world, have the responsibility and opportunity to lead in this endeavor. By recognizing the value of Indigenous communities and incorporating their knowledge into decision-making processes, we can create a future that is both environmentally and culturally sustainable.

Cultural Preservation: Fostering Indigenous Identity in the Face of Environmental Change

In the rapidly changing Arctic region, the preservation of indigenous cultures and identities is of utmost importance. As Canada and Russia capitalize on post-global warming opportunities, it is crucial that they prioritize the cultural preservation of their indigenous populations. This subchapter explores the various ways in which both countries can foster indigenous identity in the face of environmental change.

Indigenous communities have a deep connection to the land and rely on traditional knowledge for their survival. As the effects of climate change become more pronounced, it is essential to support the preservation of indigenous land management practices and traditional knowledge. By doing so, Canada and Russia can ensure the sustainability of the Arctic ecosystem and promote cultural preservation.

Furthermore, both countries can invest in research and scientific collaboration focused on climate change, adaptation strategies, and environmental preservation. By combining indigenous traditional knowledge with scientific expertise, Canada and Russia can develop innovative solutions to the challenges posed by global warming. This collaboration can also provide valuable insights to other nations facing similar challenges, promoting international cooperation in preserving indigenous cultures and protecting the environment.

In addition, Canada and Russia can develop adaptation and resilience strategies to mitigate the impacts of climate change on indigenous communities. By sharing their expertise in climate change adaptation and resilience planning, both countries can assist other nations in developing strategies to protect their indigenous populations and ensure their cultural heritage endures.

Arctic diplomacy and governance also play a significant role in fostering indigenous identity. As Canada and Russia become key players in the region, they must actively participate in shaping international agreements, regulations, and governance frameworks related to Arctic affairs. By including the perspectives and concerns of indigenous communities in these discussions, both countries can ensure that their voices are heard and their cultural preservation is prioritized.

Ultimately, Canada and Russia have a unique opportunity to lead the way in cultural preservation and indigenous identity in the face of environmental change. By supporting indigenous land management practices, investing in research and scientific collaboration, developing adaptation strategies, and actively participating in Arctic diplomacy and governance, both countries can foster cultural preservation and sustainable land-use practices for generations to come.

Sustainable Land Use Practices: Collaborating with Indigenous Communities for Long-Term Environmental Stewardship

In the rapidly changing landscape of the Arctic, it is imperative that Canada and Russia take proactive measures to ensure long-term environmental stewardship and sustainable land use practices. One crucial aspect of this effort is collaborating with indigenous communities who have lived in harmony with the Arctic environment for centuries.

Indigenous communities possess a wealth of traditional knowledge that can guide sustainable land management practices in the face of climate change. Their intimate understanding of the land, its resources, and its delicate ecosystems can provide invaluable insights for policymakers, educators, journalists, and the public.

By working hand-in-hand with indigenous communities, Canada and Russia can develop innovative strategies for resource extraction, renewable energy development, tourism, fisheries, aquaculture, infrastructure development, research, and scientific collaboration. This collaborative approach ensures that the economic opportunities presented by the post-global warming world are pursued in an environmentally conscious manner.

In the realm of resource extraction, indigenous communities can contribute to the development of responsible mining, oil and gas extraction, and other resource-based industries. Their traditional knowledge can inform sustainable practices that minimize environmental impact and respect the delicate balance of the Arctic ecosystem.

With the shift towards renewable energy sources, indigenous communities can play a vital role in harnessing the vast potential for wind, solar, and hydroelectric power generation. By involving them in the planning, implementation, and management of renewable energy projects, Canada and Russia can become leaders in clean energy production while respecting the rights and interests of indigenous peoples.

Furthermore, indigenous communities can contribute to the development of sustainable tourism and ecotourism initiatives. Their deep connection to the land and its wildlife can provide unique and authentic experiences for tourists interested in witnessing the environmental changes brought about by global warming.

In the realm of fisheries and aquaculture, indigenous communities can offer valuable insights into sustainable fishing practices and the cultivation of new species in response to shifting ecosystems. This collaboration can help Canada and Russia meet the growing global demand for seafood while ensuring the long-term health of Arctic marine ecosystems.

Moreover, indigenous communities can contribute to the development of infrastructure and shipping routes in the Arctic. Their traditional knowledge of navigation, ice conditions, and local geography can inform the construction of ports, shipping lanes, and other infrastructure projects that facilitate increased trade and transportation between Europe and Asia.

Research and scientific collaboration between indigenous communities, scientists, and policymakers can lead to a deeper understanding of climate change adaptation strategies and environmental preservation. By valuing and incorporating indigenous knowledge into research initiatives, Canada and Russia can enhance their response to the challenges posed by global warming.

In the emerging carbon offset markets, indigenous communities can play a significant role by actively participating in carbon capture and storage technologies, offering carbon credits, and engaging in emissions trading. This collaboration can provide economic opportunities while reducing greenhouse gas emissions and mitigating the effects of climate change.

Canada and Russia must also support the preservation of indigenous land management practices and traditional knowledge. By fostering cultural preservation, these nations can ensure the sustainable use of land and resources while respecting the rights and autonomy of indigenous communities.

Lastly, as economic and geopolitical interests in the Arctic region grow, Canada and Russia can play a leading role in shaping international agreements, regulations, and governance frameworks related to Arctic affairs. By prioritizing indigenous rights and environmental sustainability, both countries can contribute to the development of a robust and inclusive Arctic diplomacy and governance structure.

In conclusion, sustainable land use practices in the Arctic require collaboration with indigenous communities. By valuing their traditional knowledge, supporting cultural preservation, and involving them in decision-making processes, Canada and Russia can capitalize on the post-global warming opportunities while ensuring the long-term environmental stewardship of this unique and fragile region.

Chapter 11: Arctic diplomacy and governance

The Geopolitical Landscape of the Arctic: Canada and Russia's Role in Shaping Arctic Governance

In the rapidly changing Arctic landscape, Canada and Russia have emerged as key players in shaping the future of the region. As global warming continues to melt the ice and open up new opportunities, these two nations are capitalizing on the post-global warming world in various sectors, positioning themselves as major winners. This subchapter explores their roles in shaping Arctic governance and the potential benefits they can derive from this changing geopolitical landscape.

Arctic resource extraction is one area where both Canada and Russia can reap significant rewards. The increased accessibility of natural resources in the region, including minerals, oil, and gas, presents lucrative opportunities for mining and extraction industries. By leveraging their expertise and advanced technologies, these nations can bolster their economies and meet the growing global demand for these resources.

Another area of potential growth is renewable energy development. With their vast territories and natural resources, Canada and Russia can become leaders in wind, solar, and hydroelectric power generation. By tapping into their clean energy potential, they can not only address their own energy needs but also export excess energy to other regions, contributing to a more sustainable future.

Tourism and ecotourism in the Arctic region offer new avenues for economic growth. As the effects of global warming become more evident, Canada and Russia can attract tourists interested in witnessing the unique environmental changes and wildlife in these regions. By promoting responsible tourism practices, they can ensure the preservation of the delicate Arctic ecosystem while also generating revenue and employment opportunities.

The melting ice also opens up new fishing grounds and opportunities for aquaculture. Canada and Russia can expand their fishing industries to meet the growing global demand for seafood. By implementing sustainable fishing practices, they can ensure the long-term viability of these industries while contributing to food security and economic growth.

Infrastructure development and the opening of new Arctic shipping routes present prospects for increased trade and transportation. Canada and Russia can invest in the construction of ports and shipping lanes to facilitate the movement of goods between Europe and Asia, tapping into the potential for heightened economic activity and increased connectivity.

The changing climate in the Arctic necessitates extensive research and scientific collaboration. Canada and Russia can join forces to study climate change, adaptation strategies, and environmental preservation. By pooling their resources and knowledge, they can develop innovative solutions and inform global policies to address the challenges posed by a rapidly changing Arctic environment.

Both nations can also benefit from emerging carbon offset markets and emissions trading. By investing in carbon capture and storage technologies, offering carbon credits, and participating in emissions trading, Canada and Russia can take advantage of this new economic landscape while actively contributing to the fight against climate change.

As global warming intensifies, adaptation and resilience strategies become crucial. Canada and Russia can develop and export their expertise in climate change adaptation and resilience planning to other nations facing similar challenges. By sharing best practices and working together, they can create a more resilient future for all.

Preserving indigenous land management practices and traditional knowledge is of paramount importance as the Arctic undergoes rapid changes. Canada and Russia can support indigenous communities in preserving their cultural heritage and sustainable land-use practices. By recognizing and integrating traditional knowledge into decision-making processes, they can foster cultural preservation and ensure the sustainable development of the Arctic.

Lastly, with their economic and geopolitical interests in the Arctic, Canada and Russia can play a significant role in shaping international agreements, regulations, and governance frameworks related to Arctic affairs. By actively participating in Arctic diplomacy, they can influence the establishment of fair and effective governance structures, ensuring the long-term sustainability and stability of the region.

In conclusion, Canada and Russia are poised to capitalize on the post-global warming opportunities in the Arctic. Through resource extraction, renewable energy development, tourism, fisheries, infrastructure development, research collaboration, carbon offset markets, adaptation strategies, indigenous land management, and Arctic governance, these nations can shape the future of the region while reaping significant economic and geopolitical rewards. However, the sustainability of these endeavors must be prioritized to ensure the long-term well-being of the Arctic and its inhabitants.

International Agreements: Navigating the Complexities of Arctic Diplomacy

In the rapidly changing landscape of the Arctic, international agreements play a crucial role in shaping the future of the region. As Canada and Russia emerge as the big winners in the post-global warming world, it is essential for politicians, educators, journalists, and the public to understand the complexities of Arctic diplomacy and the opportunities it presents.

Arctic resource extraction is a key area where Canada and Russia can capitalize on the increased accessibility of natural resources due to melting ice. With vast reserves of minerals, oil, and gas, both countries have the potential to boost their mining, oil and gas extraction, and other resource-based industries, driving economic growth and prosperity.

Another area of opportunity lies in renewable energy development. With the global shift towards clean energy sources, Canada and Russia can harness their vast potential for wind, solar, and hydroelectric power generation. By becoming leaders in clean energy production, both countries can not only meet their own energy demands but also contribute to a greener and more sustainable future.

Tourism and ecotourism also hold immense potential in the Arctic regions. As the effects of global warming become more evident, Canada and Russia can attract tourists interested in witnessing the unique environmental changes and wildlife in the Arctic. By promoting responsible tourism practices, both countries can ensure the preservation of this fragile ecosystem while benefiting from the economic opportunities it presents.

The melting Arctic ice also opens up new fishing grounds and opportunities for aquaculture. Canada and Russia can expand their fishing industries to meet the growing global demand for seafood. By implementing sustainable fishing practices, both countries can ensure the long-term viability of this valuable resource.

Infrastructure development and shipping routes in the Arctic are another area of focus. With the opening of new Arctic shipping routes,

Canada and Russia can invest in infrastructure, such as ports and shipping lanes, to facilitate increased trade and transportation between Europe and Asia. This will not only boost economic activity but also enhance connectivity between regions.

Research and scientific collaboration are crucial for understanding and mitigating the effects of climate change in the Arctic. Canada and Russia can collaborate on research initiatives focused on climate change, adaptation strategies, and environmental preservation. By sharing knowledge and expertise, both countries can contribute to global efforts to combat climate change.

Carbon offset markets and emissions trading present additional opportunities for Canada and Russia. By investing in carbon capture and storage technologies, offering carbon credits, and participating in emissions trading, both countries can take advantage of the emerging carbon offset markets, contributing to global efforts to reduce greenhouse gas emissions.

As the effects of global warming become more pronounced, Canada and Russia can develop and export expertise in climate change adaptation and resilience planning. By sharing their knowledge and strategies, they can assist other nations facing similar challenges, fostering global collaboration in addressing the impacts of climate change.

Preserving indigenous land management practices and traditional knowledge is of utmost importance in the face of climate change. Canada and Russia can support indigenous communities in maintaining their cultural heritage and sustainable land-use practices. By valuing and incorporating indigenous knowledge, both countries can achieve a more holistic approach to environmental stewardship.

Arctic diplomacy and governance are vital in shaping international agreements, regulations, and governance frameworks related to Arctic affairs. Canada and Russia, as key players in the region, can play a significant role in ensuring responsible and sustainable development while safeguarding the interests of all stakeholders.

In conclusion, navigating the complexities of Arctic diplomacy is essential for Canada and Russia to capitalize on the post-global warming opportunities. From resource extraction to renewable energy development, tourism to fisheries, infrastructure to research collaboration, carbon offset markets to adaptation strategies, and indigenous land management to Arctic governance, there are numerous avenues for these countries to secure their positions as leaders in the changing Arctic landscape. By engaging in international agreements and forging strong partnerships, they can pave the way for a sustainable and prosperous future in the Arctic.

Regulations and Governance Frameworks: Ensuring Sustainable Development in the Arctic

The Arctic region is undergoing significant changes due to global warming, and both Canada and Russia are poised to capitalize on the opportunities that arise as a result. However, it is crucial to ensure that the development in the Arctic is sustainable and takes into account the unique environmental and ecological characteristics of the region. This subchapter explores the importance of regulations and governance frameworks in achieving this goal.

As politicians, educators, journalists, and the public, it is essential to understand the various aspects of sustainable development in the Arctic and the role that regulations and governance frameworks play in this process.

Arctic resource extraction is one area where regulations are crucial. With the increased accessibility of natural resources in the Arctic, both Canada and Russia have the potential to benefit from mining, oil and gas extraction, and other resource-based industries. However, it is essential to have robust regulations in place to ensure responsible and sustainable extraction practices that minimize environmental impact.

Similarly, renewable energy development holds immense potential in the Arctic. Both Canada and Russia can tap into their vast resources for wind, solar, and hydroelectric power generation, becoming leaders in clean energy production. However, regulations and governance frameworks are necessary to promote the transition to renewable energy sources and ensure that development is conducted in an environmentally friendly manner.

Tourism and ecotourism are also areas where regulations are crucial. As the effects of global warming become more evident, Canada and Russia can attract tourists interested in witnessing the unique environmental changes and wildlife in the Arctic regions. However, regulations must be in place to protect fragile ecosystems, ensure responsible tourism practices, and minimize the impact on indigenous communities.

The melting Arctic ice also opens up new opportunities for fisheries and aquaculture. Canada and Russia can expand their fishing industries and meet the growing global demand for seafood. However, regulations are essential to ensure sustainable fishing practices and prevent overfishing.

Infrastructure development and shipping routes are another aspect that requires regulations and governance frameworks. With the opening of new Arctic shipping routes, Canada and Russia can invest in infrastructure development to facilitate increased trade and transportation. However, regulations must be in place to protect the fragile Arctic environment and prevent accidents and spills.

Research and scientific collaboration are crucial in understanding and mitigating the effects of climate change in the Arctic. Canada and Russia can collaborate on research initiatives focused on climate change, adaptation strategies, and environmental preservation. Regulations and governance frameworks are necessary to encourage and facilitate such collaborations.

Carbon offset markets and emissions trading offer opportunities for both Canada and Russia to invest in carbon capture and storage technologies and participate in emissions trading. Regulations and governance frameworks are crucial to ensure the integrity and effectiveness of these markets.

Adaptation and resilience strategies are vital in the face of global warming. Canada and Russia can develop and export expertise in climate change adaptation and resilience planning to other nations facing similar challenges. Regulations and governance frameworks can support and promote these strategies.

Preserving indigenous land management practices and traditional knowledge is of utmost importance in the face of climate change. Canada and Russia can support the preservation of indigenous knowledge, fostering cultural preservation and sustainable land-use practices. Regulations and governance frameworks can play a vital role in protecting indigenous rights and promoting their inclusion in decision-making processes.

Finally, as economic and geopolitical interests in the Arctic region increase, Canada and Russia can play a significant role in shaping international agreements, regulations, and governance frameworks related to Arctic affairs. Their leadership can ensure that sustainable development and environmental protection are at the forefront of Arctic diplomacy.

In conclusion, regulations and governance frameworks are crucial in ensuring sustainable development in the Arctic. From resource extraction to renewable energy, tourism to fisheries, infrastructure to research, adaptation to indigenous land management, and Arctic diplomacy, robust regulations are essential to protect the fragile Arctic environment and promote sustainable practices. As politicians, educators, journalists, and the public, it is our responsibility to advocate for and support the development and implementation of these regulations and governance frameworks to secure a sustainable future for the Arctic.

Conclusion: Seizing the Opportunities: Canada and Russia as Leaders in the Post-Global Warming Arctic World

In this book, "The Arctic Boom: How Canada and Russia are Capitalizing on Post-Global Warming Opportunities," we have explored the immense potential for Canada and Russia to emerge as leaders in the post-global warming Arctic world. The effects of climate change have led to unprecedented changes in the Arctic region, creating new opportunities for economic growth, innovation, and collaboration. As we conclude our exploration, it becomes clear that both Canada and Russia have the resources, expertise, and strategic positioning to capitalize on these opportunities and shape the future of the Arctic.

Arctic resource extraction presents a significant opportunity for both countries. With the melting ice opening up new areas for mining, oil and gas extraction, and other resource-based industries, Canada and Russia can tap into vast natural resources. By responsibly developing these resources, they can not only meet the growing global demand but also stimulate economic growth and create employment opportunities for their citizens.

The shift towards renewable energy sources offers another avenue for leadership. Canada and Russia possess immense potential for wind, solar, and hydroelectric power generation. By investing in renewable energy development, both countries can become pioneers in clean energy production, reducing their dependence on fossil fuels and mitigating the impact of climate change.

Tourism and ecotourism are also on the rise in the Arctic regions. As global warming causes unique environmental changes, Canada and Russia can attract tourists interested in witnessing these transformations and the abundant wildlife in the Arctic. By promoting sustainable tourism practices, they can not only boost their economies but also raise awareness about the importance of preserving the fragile Arctic ecosystem.

The melting Arctic ice also presents new opportunities for fisheries and aquaculture. Canada and Russia can expand their fishing industries and meet the growing global demand for seafood by utilizing the emerging fishing grounds and engaging in responsible aquaculture practices.

Infrastructure development and the opening of new Arctic shipping routes offer immense potential for increased trade and transportation between Europe and Asia. By investing in ports and shipping lanes, Canada and Russia can facilitate this trade, strengthening their economic ties and positioning themselves as key players in global commerce.

Collaboration on research initiatives focused on climate change, adaptation strategies, and environmental preservation is another area where Canada and Russia can lead. By pooling their resources and expertise, they can address the challenges posed by the changing climate in the Arctic and contribute to global efforts to combat climate change.

Both countries can also take advantage of carbon offset markets and emissions trading. By investing in carbon capture and storage technologies, offering carbon credits, and participating in emissions trading, Canada and Russia can not only reduce their carbon footprint but also generate revenue and stimulate economic growth.

As the effects of global warming become more pronounced, Canada and Russia can develop and export expertise in climate change adaptation and resilience planning. By sharing their knowledge and experiences, they can assist other nations facing similar challenges and foster sustainable development worldwide.

Furthermore, both countries have the opportunity to support the preservation of indigenous land management practices and traditional knowledge. By working closely with indigenous communities, Canada and Russia can foster cultural preservation, sustainable land-use practices, and a deeper understanding of the Arctic ecosystem.

Lastly, with increased economic and geopolitical interests in the Arctic region, Canada and Russia can play a significant role in shaping international agreements, regulations, and governance frameworks related to Arctic affairs. By engaging in Arctic diplomacy, they can ensure that the region is managed sustainably and in the best interests of all stakeholders.

In conclusion, Canada and Russia are well-positioned to seize the opportunities presented by the post-global warming Arctic world. By capitalizing on their natural resources, investing in renewable energy, promoting sustainable tourism, expanding fisheries and aquaculture, developing infrastructure, collaborating on research, participating in carbon offset markets, promoting adaptation and resilience strategies, supporting indigenous land management, and engaging in Arctic diplomacy, they can establish themselves as leaders in this rapidly changing region. The future of the Arctic lies in their hands, and it is up to them to shape it responsibly and sustainably.